P9-DFQ-728

What Cats Teach Us...

LIFE'S LESSONS LEARNED FROM OUR FELINE FRIENDS

GLENN DROMGOOLE

WILLOW CREEK PRESS
Minocqua, Wisconsin

© 2000 Glenn Dromgoole

Published by Willow Creek Press
P.O. Box 147
Minocqua, Wisconsin 54548

For information on other Willow Creek titles, call 1-800-850-9453

**Library of Congress
Cataloging-in-Publication Data**

Dromgoole, Glenn.
    What cats teach us-- : life's lessons
    learned from our feline friends / by Glenn
    Dromgoole
        p.   cm.
    ISBN 1-57223-296-X

Printed in Canada

PHOTOGRAPHER CREDITS

Norvia Behling: pages 6, 8, 15, 16, 22, 41, 46, 49, 51, 54, 59, 68, 69, 72, 77, 80, 81, 89, 98, 111.
Ron Kimball: pages 7, 12, 13, 14, 23, 29, 37, 38, 39, 40, 47, 58, 63, 64, 83, 85, 88, 92, 100.
Alan & Sandy Carey: pages 10, 11, 20, 44, 55, 56, 60, 79, 82, 90, 91, 97, 103, 107, 109, 110, 112.
Louisa Preston: pages 9, 26, 35, 50, 52, 67, 86.
Paulette Braun: pages 17, 61, 84, 95, 101.
Sharon Eide: pages 18, 24, 71, 87, 105.
B & C Beck Photo: page 19.
Daniel Johnson: page 21
Bonnie Nance: pages 25, 28, 30, 31, 32, 33, 36, 42, 43, 45, 62, 74, 78, 94, 96, 99, 104, 106, 108.
Dale C. Spartas: page 34.
Elizabeth Flynn: page 48.
Diane Ensign/www.greenagency.net: page 53.
Bonnie Sue: page 65.
Bob Firth/Firth Photobank: page: 66, 76, 102.
The Terry Wild Studio: page 70
Kent & Donna Dannen: page 73.

Table of Contents

Acknowledgments

Carol Dromgoole, Jennifer LeBow, Russ Lackey, Charlie Hukill, Betty Hukill, Jeff Wolf, and Sue Wolf contributed valuable insights and suggestions from their experiences with Tiptoe, Sunshine, C.C., Max, Rita, Willie, Boots, Theo, and Squeaky.

About Healthy Living

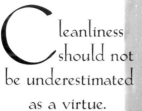

Cleanliness
should not
be underestimated
as a virtue.

Stretch real good the first thing every morning—
and every other chance you get.

When you can lie in the sunshine, do so.

Gaze out the window a lot.

Good grooming is an asset.

Don't have more babies than you can provide for.

I sure helps to get a soft hug
at the end of a hard day.

There's no better time for a quick nap than right now.

Conserve your energy for when it counts.

Get a
thorough
physical exam
at least once
a year.

Follow your instincts.

WHAT CATS TEACH US

The best cure for insomnia is sleep.

Drink plenty of water.

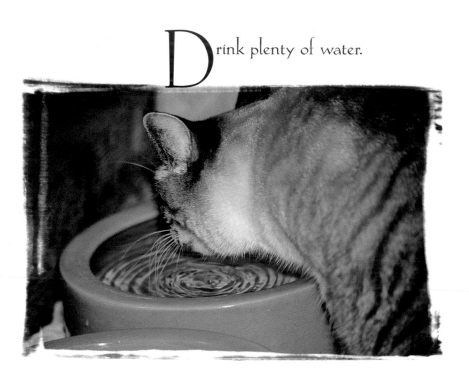

$\mathcal{S}$cratch what itches.

W hen
you have
an opportunity
to go to the
bathroom, do so.

Be careful in traffic.

Eat a balanced diet.

WHAT CATS TEACH US

There are times when we just have to take a leap of faith.

Always be happy about getting a special treat.

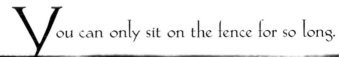

You can only sit on the fence for so long.

Always wash up before dinner.

About Getting Along with Others

Don't hesitate to show affection to those you love.

WHAT CATS TEACH US

I't's good to be pampered.

Never underestimate the power of a purr.

The world
could always use
a little more
gentleness.

T

ake time to play with the people you love.

Pay close
attention to
one person
at a time.

If someone offers to scratch your back, let them.

Be thankful that someone took care of you when you were too little to fend for yourself.

Make
someone else
feel better
by giving them
a few strokes.

WHAT CATS TEACH US

Make eye contact if you want something.

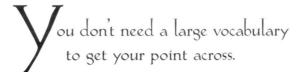

You don't need a large vocabulary
to get your point across.

WHAT CATS TEACH US

We have to trust somebody sometime.

Do not suffer fools gladly.

Understand
that no one
owns you.

Enjoy the
company of
children …

WHAT CATS TEACH US

and older people.

You don't have
to be rich or
famous or
powerful
to be loved.

Look forward to someone
you love coming home.

K

eep an eye on your enemies . . .

and trust
your
friends.

Don't be too critical of your friends.

WHAT CATS TEACH US

hare what
you have
with others.

Always appreciate a friend who listens.

WHAT CATS TEACH US

T ake comfort in the kindness of strangers.

Faithfulness is a basic ingredient of a loving relationship.

WHAT CATS TEACH US

Make companionship a priority.

Don't pick on those in less fortunate situations.

WHAT CATS TEACH US

Nobody understands like your mom.

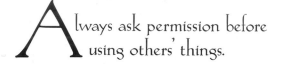

Always ask permission before using others' things.

What Cats Teach Us

About
Self-Esteem

It enhances your reputation if you're a little mysterious.

WHAT CATS TEACH US

B ullies usually won't bother you if you bow
your back and stand your ground.

Running away from a fight may be a sign of intelligence, not cowardice.

WHAT CATS TEACH US

When
you want to get
to a high place,
have confidence
in your ability
to get there.

Sophisticated laziness does not come naturally;
you have to cultivate it.

WHAT CATS TEACH US

E ven if you know you're superior to everyone in the room, don't gloat.

$\mathcal{Y}$ou'll never get anywhere running in circles.

WHAT CATS TEACH US

Be proud of your unique attributes.

E ven if
you
sing
poorly,
sing.

WHAT CATS TEACH US

Everyone gets down sometimes.

B_e
happy with
who you are.

What Cats Teach Us

The ability to laugh at yourself is priceless.

Being kind is more important
than being important.

WHAT CATS TEACH US

S ometimes it's best to hold your tongue.

Count to ten before scolding.

WHAT CATS TEACH US

Contentment is as fine a goal as any.

A little peace and quiet will calm both you and your soul.

WHAT CATS TEACH US

About
Self-
Improvement

L earn
to keep
your cool
in difficult
situations.

WHAT CATS TEACH US

If an opportunity
presents itself,
   pounce on it.

Y ou can learn a lot if you keep quiet and listen.

WHAT CATS TEACH US

Nurture your independent spirit.

Express your individuality.

D on't stifle
your curiosity.

Don't go out on a limb unless you're forced to.

WHAT CATS TEACH US

Keep
up your
appearance.

However many lives we may think we have, this is the one we need to make the most of.

WHAT CATS TEACH US

I f you spend too much time watching
the world go by, it will.

Never, ever drink out of toilets.

What Cats Teach Us

Be curious about what's on the other side of the fence, but try to avoid jealousy.

$\int$ tay quietly focused on the task at hand.

WHAT CATS TEACH US

$\mathbb{A}$ll creatures on earth should be respected.

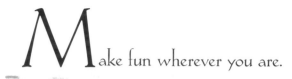

Make fun wherever you are.

WHAT CATS TEACH US

Taking risks can lead to unexpected but beautiful new perspectives.

$\int$ avor those moments when you can be alone.

What Cats Teach Us

About
Everyday
Living

Avoid fights.

I's important
to know your
way home.

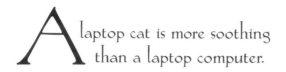

A laptop cat is more soothing
than a laptop computer.

WHAT CATS TEACH US

Find a special spot and spend a lot of time there.

I f you can't lie on a piece of furniture, what's the point in having it?

Support humane causes.

It's hard to get in trouble when you're asleep.

WHAT CATS TEACH US

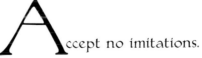

Accept no imitations.

We can't always get what we want.

Most of the time, our problems are self-created.

We all need to spend some time alone.

Be quick to seize opportunity.

H iding under the covers won't make your problems disappear.

WHAT CATS TEACH US

Give in
and
accept help in
an impossible
situation.

Don't be afraid of the world;
     it's not as big as it seems.

WHAT CATS TEACH US

Listen to
your parents
and you won't
get into so
much trouble.

E very day has its challenges . . .

WHAT CATS TEACH US

and its joys.

Bask in the beauty of the world around you.

WHAT CATS TEACH US